Epidemics can start off slowly.
One person gets sick. Then a neighbor.
Then lots of people around town. The
next thing you know, hospitals are packed.
Everyone is terrified of being infected.

The Virus

That's what experts feared could be happening in New York City. Six people in the same neighborhood had come down with a rare virus that attacks the brain.

And that wasn't all. In another part of the city, the flamingos at the Bronx Zoo had dropped dead.

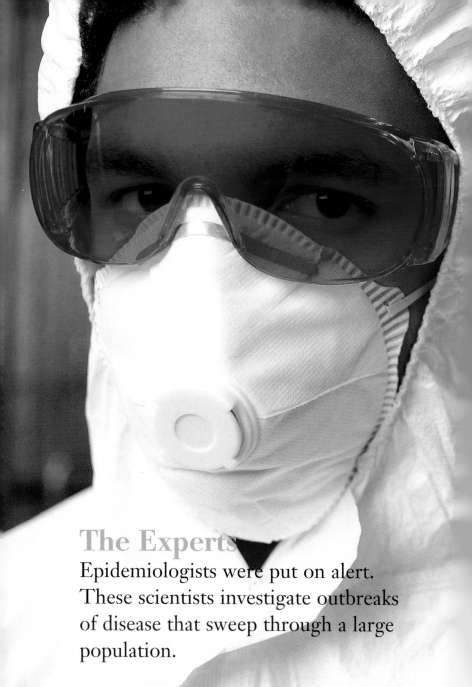

The Experts

Epidemiologists were put on alert. These scientists investigate outbreaks of disease that sweep through a large population.

The Question

How would epidemiologists determine whether there was a connection between the sick New Yorkers and the dead birds? Are epidemics more or less likely to occur today than they were in the past?

Cover design: Maria Bergós, Book&Look **Interior design:** Red Herring Design/NYC

Photo Credits ©: cover top mosquitoes: Anne Cusack/Los Angeles Times/Getty Images; cover scientist: D-Keine/Getty Images; cover skyline: franckreporter/Getty Images; 1: Jonathan Torgovnik/Getty Images; 4-5: Media Bakery; 8: David Scharf/Science Source; 10: David Sacks/Getty Images; 13: Darren McCollester/Getty Images; 14 top: James Gathany/ Centers for Disease Control and Prevention; 15 bottom: Greg Knobloch/Centers for Disease Control and Prevention; 16: Airelle-Joubert/Science Source; 21: James Leynse/Corbis/Getty Images; 22-23: Centers for Disease Control and Prevention; 23 bottom: Red Herring; 30: Chris Johns/National Geographic Creative; 33: Sparky/Getty Images; 34: Pascal Goetgheluck/ Science Source; 35: 3D4Medical/Science Source; 36 right top: Anest/Dreamstime; 36 right center, right bottom: James Gathany/Centers for Disease Control and Prevention; 36 bottom: Biophoto Associates/Science Source; 37: Clouds Hill Imaging Ltd./Science Source; 38: Courtesy of Sarah Wheeler; 39: Pete Oxford/Minden Pictures; 40 left: Zsv3207/ Dreamstime; 40 right: Faith O'Connor/Alamy Images; 41 top left: Jim Bolt/AP Images; 41 bottom: Dan Currier/Getty Images; 43 left inset: Larry West/Science Source; 43 right: London School of Hygiene & Tropical Medicine/Science Source.

All other photos © Shutterstock.

With thanks to John DiConsiglio

Library of Congress Cataloging-in-Publication Data
Names: Shea, John, 1966- author.
Title: Bitten! : mosquitoes infect New York / John Shea.
Description: [New edition] | New York : Children's Press, 2020. | Series: Xbooks | Originally published:
New York : Scholastic, ©2012 | Audience: Ages 8-10. | Audience: Grades 4-6. | Summary:
"Book introduces the reader to mosquitoes"-- Provided by publisher.
Identifiers: LCCN 2020008049 | ISBN 9780531132333 (library binding) | ISBN 9780531132982 (paperback)
Subjects: LCSH: Mosquitoes as carriers of disease--New York (State)--New York--Juvenile literature.
| Insects as carriers of disease--New York (State)--New York--Juvenile literature.
| West Nile virus--New York (State)--New York--Juvenile literature.
Classification: LCC RA640 .S53 2020 | DDC 614.4/323097471--dc23
LC record available at https://lccn.loc.gov/2020008049

No part of this publication may be reproduced in whole or in part, or stored in a retrieval system, or transmitted in any form or by any means, electronic, mechanical, photocopying, recording, or otherwise, without written permission of the publisher. For information regarding permission, write to Scholastic Inc., Attention: Permissions Department, Scholastic Inc., 557 Broadway, New York, NY 10012.

© 2021, 2012, 2008 Scholastic Inc.

All rights reserved. Published by Scholastic Inc.

Printed in Johor Bahru, Malaysia   108

1 2 3 4 5 6 7 8 9 10 R 30 29 28 27 26 25 24 23 22 21

SCHOLASTIC, XBOOKS, and associated logos are trademarks and/or registered trademarks of Scholastic Inc.

Scholastic Inc., 557 Broadway, New York, NY 10012.

BITTEN!

Mosquitoes Infect
New York

JOHN SHEA

SCHOLASTIC

FEMALE MOSQUITOES have a long mouthpart, called a proboscis, that can pierce the skin and suck up blood.

TABLE OF CONTENTS

PREVIEW 1

CHAPTER 1
Outbreak! 10
A mystery illness strikes in New York City.

Outbreak Central 14

CHAPTER 2
Search for the Vector 16
Scientists investigate a mysterious virus. Meanwhile, a killer is on the loose.

Meet the Mosquito 22

CHAPTER 3
The Missing Link 24
Is there a link between the sick people and the dead birds?

West Nile Virus: Fact Versus Fiction 28

CHAPTER 4
Coast to Coast 30
Is there any way to stop West Nile virus?

Close-Up on the *Culex* ... 36

XFILES 37

Bird-Watcher 38

Skeeter Shooting 40

Kill the Carrier 42

1

Outbreak!

A mystery illness strikes in New York City.

When the phone rings in Dr. Ned Hayes's office, it is not likely to be about a single sick person. Usually it is about lots of people affected by an illness.

Hayes is an epidemiologist at the Centers for Disease Control and Prevention (CDC). Epidemiologists investigate epidemics—outbreaks of disease that infect large numbers of people. They study and try to stop infectious diseases. Those are diseases that are spread through water, food, air, body fluids, or by carriers such as insects and birds.

In 1999, Hayes got a somewhat unusual call. In New York City, people were coming down with a strange virus. And it appeared that they had caught the virus from mosquitoes.

That was exactly the kind of case that set Hayes abuzz. Diseases that are spread by insects or other living things are known as vector-borne illnesses. Hayes is a specialist in vector-borne diseases spread by insects. If insects are making people sick, it's up to Hayes to step in before whole communities—or even whole countries—become infected.

Would Hayes be able to save New York City from falling prey to deadly mosquitoes?

A RESEARCHER EXAMINES a mosquito suspected of carrying a virus. Viruses can grow and reproduce only inside the cells of living things. They can cause many serious diseases.

Outbreak Central

The CDC headquarters in Atlanta, Georgia

The CDC has a long history of tracking epidemics in the U.S. and around the world.

"You may not know our name," a worker at the CDC says. "But you hear from us when an outbreak occurs and a quick response is needed."

The CDC is the U.S. government agency that fights epidemics. Here's a quick look at some of the epidemics it has investigated.

1946   **1950**   **195?**

1950: The CDC studies polio in Ohio. The polio virus attacks the nerves and causes paralysis.

1946: The CDC is formed. Its first mission is to wipe out malaria in the U.S. Malaria is an infectious disease carried by mosquitoes.

1953: The CDC reports the first case of rabies in a bat. Rabies is spread mainly by infected animals.

1954: The CDC begins studying leptospirosis. This disease is spread by drinking water that has been contaminated by urine from an infected animal.

1989: The CDC reports that guns are the eighth-leading cause of death in the U.S., qualifying gun violence as an epidemic and a threat to public health.

1958: A CDC team goes to Southeast Asia to help with two epidemics: cholera, which attacks the small intestine, and small-pox, which causes blisters on the skin.

2020: The CDC monitors and responds to the outbreak of a respiratory disease (COVID-19) caused by a new corona-virus. The virus was first detected in China in 2019, and it quickly turned into a pandemic with global effects.

1954   1958   1976   1989   2008 2020

A CDC RESEARCHER does a test on an egg infected with a flu virus.

2008: The CDC monitors huge outbreaks of food-borne illnesses.

1976: The CDC investigates outbreaks of the Ebola virus in the African countries of Zaire and Sudan. Ebola causes massive internal bleeding.

15

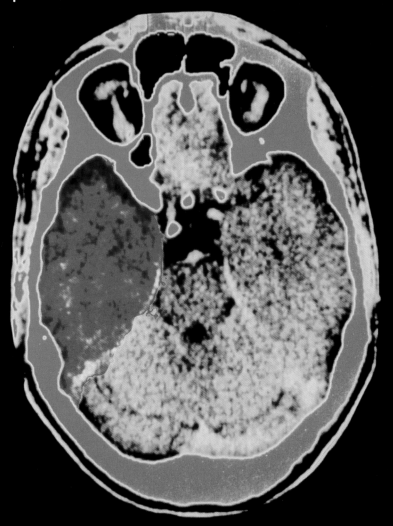

THIS BRAIN SCAN shows encephalitis (red area) on the left side of a person's brain.

2

Search for the Vector

Scientists investigate a mysterious virus. Meanwhile, a killer is on the loose.

Dr. Ned Hayes met with his colleagues at the CDC. The CDC monitors epidemics and other events that threaten public health.

The CDC scientists were perplexed. Doctors in New York City were reporting mysterious cases of encephalitis. That's the term for a dangerous inflammation, or swelling, of the brain. It's often fatal. One doctor saw two cases in a matter of days. And six cases were reported in the same neighborhood.

Viruses

Encephalitis can be caused by a virus. Viruses are extremely tiny. They grow and reproduce inside the cells of a host plant or animal. There are thousands of kinds of viruses. If the conditions are right, they can cause serious diseases in their hosts.

The doctors in New York tested the sick patients for the viruses that most commonly cause encephalitis. The patients' test results were negative for those viruses. That meant that they had been infected by a more unusual virus.

But how had they gotten the virus? Many of the infected patients lived near each other. The New York doctors suspected that they had all been infected by the same vector—or carrier—of the virus. That vector was most likely mosquitoes.

Scientists at the CDC asked the New York City Health Department for the patients' blood samples. These samples were tested. Results showed that the New Yorkers were indeed suffering from a mosquito-borne virus.

Disease Cycle

The patients appeared to have a viral disease called St. Louis encephalitis. It's carried by mosquitoes that belong to a group known as *Culex*.

The mosquitoes get the virus by feeding on infected birds. Then the infected mosquitoes pass the virus on to humans. Typically, neither birds nor mosquitoes are harmed by the St. Louis virus. Most people don't suffer any symptoms either. But the virus can cause headaches and fevers in some people. And some people, especially the elderly, can get very sick.

Hayes and the other scientists at the CDC were stunned. In the previous 40 years, there had been fewer than 5,000 cases of St. Louis encephalitis—and none in New York City. They wondered, why was there a sudden outbreak?

The CDC had a mystery on its hands. How had so many people come down with the same rare disease?

Bird Killer

Before the scientists could take a guess, the mystery deepened. At about the same time that the virus started infecting people in New York, another phone rang in the offices of the CDC.

A veterinarian at New York City's Bronx Zoo had troubling news. Some of the flamingos in the zoo's birdhouse had died. Corpses of other birds also littered the grounds of the zoo. And they all tested positive for a mosquito-borne virus!

Was the killer virus at the zoo related to the virus that had infected the New Yorkers?

THESE BIRDS in New York were killed by the same virus that killed the birds in the Bronx Zoo.

Meet the Mos

The mosquito is a vector for some nasty diseases. Here's everything you ever wanted to know about it—and more!

ADULT FEMALE MOSQUITO Did you know that only female mosquitoes bite? They need the protein found in blood to produce eggs. (Male mosquitoes eat plant nectar.)

thorax Along with the head and abdomen, this is one of the three main sections of an insect. Scientists look at patterns on the thorax to tell what kind of mosquito they are looking at.

abdomen This is the rear section of the mosquito. It has eight pairs of airholes. The mosquito breathes through them.

legs The mosquito has six legs that are attached to the thorax. Each leg has a pair of tiny claws that help the mosquito cling to surfaces.

quito

proboscis This long mouthpart can break through an animal's skin. There are two tubes inside it. One tube injects a painkiller so the animal can't feel the bite. The other sucks in the animal's blood. Parasites or viruses are injected into the victim's blood when an infected mosquito bites. That's how diseases get from the mosquito to its victim.

antennae These can detect an animal's breath from 100 feet (30 meters) away. Mosquitoes are attracted to carbon dioxide, a gas that people exhale. They can also detect body odors—like the smell of sweat—and the body heat that people give off.

head There is one eye on each side of the head. Each eye has many lenses that point in different directions.

wings The mosquito's two wings are attached to the thorax.

THE LIFE CYCLE OF A MOSQUITO

eggs Females lay 40 to 400 eggs in water. The eggs float together like a raft.

larvae After about two days, the eggs hatch into larvae. A larva molts (sheds its skin) four times as it grows.

pupae During their fourth molt, larvae enter their pupal stage. The pupae grow for about two days. Then the pupa's skin splits open and the adult mosquito comes out.

THIS IS AN ILLUSTRATION
of the West Nile virus.

3

The Missing Link

Is there a link between the sick people and the dead birds?

The scientists at the CDC were stumped. It seemed like too much of a coincidence for birds and humans to get sick with mosquito-borne viruses at the same time. But it also didn't seem possible for those viruses to be related. After all, the humans had been diagnosed with St. Louis virus. And that virus doesn't kill birds!

Perhaps whatever was killing the birds at the Bronx Zoo was something different than the virus that was making New Yorkers sick.

Ned Hayes and the other scientists had to figure out what virus had killed the birds at the zoo.

West Nile Virus

It was time to reach out for more help. Veterinarians at the Bronx Zoo sent the dead birds to the U.S. Department of Agriculture (USDA). The USDA can test for any mosquito-related disease.

A few days later, the test results were in. The birds tested positive for West Nile virus. West Nile was first discovered in 1937 in Uganda, a country in Africa. It is where the Nile River begins. The disease had never been seen in the United States before.

Carefully, scientists began to unravel the mystery. They discovered that the blood tests done on the sick New Yorkers had not been interpreted correctly. The patients hadn't been infected by St. Louis virus. Like the birds, they had West Nile virus. The virus had probably infected the birds first. Then mosquitoes fed on the infected birds and passed the virus on to humans. The virus was fatal to birds. But the humans had a chance for recovery.

SCIENTISTS discovered that birds and humans were infected with the same virus.

West Nile Virus: Fact Versus Fiction

West Nile virus has raced across the United States since it arrived in 1999. Learn the truth about this unwelcome visitor.

Fiction: Kids have the greatest risk of getting sick from West Nile.

Fact: Most kids who get West Nile don't develop any symptoms. People over age 50 are at the highest risk.

Fiction: You can get West Nile from sick birds.

Fact: There's no proof that humans can get West Nile directly from birds. But you shouldn't touch a sick or dead bird, just in case.

Fiction: West Nile is usually fatal.

Fact: West Nile is rarely fatal to humans. In fact, most infected people never realize that they have the virus. CDC officials think that about three million Americans have gotten the disease. About 1 in 5 people who are infected develop a fever and other symptoms. About 1 out of 150 infected people develop a serious, sometimes fatal, illness.

Fiction: You have to stay indoors to be safe from mosquitoes.

Fact: The CDC says that mosquito repellents that contain the chemicals DEET or Picaridin are effective. People who want to avoid chemicals can use repellents that contain oil of lemon eucalyptus.

Fiction: After a few years, West Nile will die out.

Fact: The only known way to wipe out West Nile is to kill all its hosts (birds) and all its vectors (mosquitoes). That's not going to happen. So the virus will probably be around for a long time.

Here are a few things you can do to avoid getting a mosquito-borne illness:

Make sure your doors and windows have tight-fitting screens with no holes.

Mosquitoes are most active in the evening. If you go outside then, wear loose-fitting clothes that cover your arms and legs.

Use mosquito repellent.

Standing water is the perfect place for mosquitoes to breed. Empty water from flowerpots, pet dishes, and birdbaths.

A MOSQUITO LANDS
by the eye of a bird.

4

Coast to Coast

Is there any way to stop West Nile virus?

How did West Nile virus get to the United States? Dr. Hayes says we may never know for sure.

Possibly an infected mosquito hitched a ride on an airplane. Or a diseased bird could have ended up in New York. "All it would take is one mosquito and one bird to find each other for the whole transmission cycle to begin," says Hayes.

There were many more questions to answer. Scientists wanted to find out how many New Yorkers were infected with the West Nile virus. To answer that question, Hayes had to gather more information. The CDC organized a survey of New Yorkers to find out how many of them were sick with West Nile.

Surveyors went door-to-door to hundreds of homes in New York. They asked whether anyone at the address had been sick recently. If so, what were their symptoms? Had they been near any dead birds?

Going Viral

The next question for Hayes was just as important. Was it possible to stop the virus from spreading? The results of the CDC's survey suggested that more than 8,000 New Yorkers were infected with West Nile virus. Birds in the nearby states of Connecticut, New Jersey, and Maryland also tested positive, fueling fears that the virus was on the move.

"We sat back and realized the scope of what we had," Hayes says. "There was a new virus in our ecosystem."

Over the next few years, Hayes and a team of scientists watched West Nile spread across the United States. For a time, states in the South and Midwest appeared to be hardest hit. "Right now, it's

A SCIENTIST looks into a breeding cage full of *Culex pipiens* mosquitoes. This type of mosquito can spread West Nile virus.

endemic to the United States," Hayes says. That means the virus will always be here. Scientists believe it will flare up during the summer and fall every year.

Killer on the Loose

Is there a cure for West Nile? No. Scientists have created a drug that protects horses from the virus, but it's not safe for humans to use. For now, scientists work with public-health groups to teach Americans about West Nile. "Our best strategy is prevention," Hayes says. "We can't kill the mosquito. We can't kill the virus. The only thing we can do is teach people how not to get sick." **X**

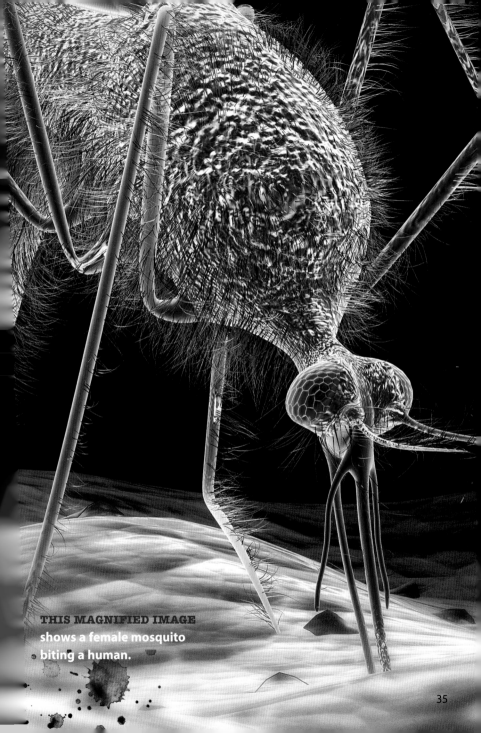

THIS MAGNIFIED IMAGE
shows a female mosquito
biting a human.

Close-Up on the *Culex*

This mosquito has a short life. But it's a major pest.

In the United States, West Nile virus is spread mostly by *Culex* mosquitoes. They usually are active during the summer months. The females can hibernate through winter in warm, sheltered areas like garages, barns, or houses. They return the next summer and lay more eggs.

These three species, or kinds, of *Culex* are some of the the most common vectors of West Nile virus.

Culex pipiens

In the northeastern U.S., the main carrier is *Culex pipiens*. It feeds on birds and mammals.

Culex quinquefasciatus

An important vector in the South is *Culex quinquefasciatus*, or the southern house mosquito.

Culex tarsalis

In the West, *Culex tarsalis* dominates. This mosquito breeds in irrigated farmland.

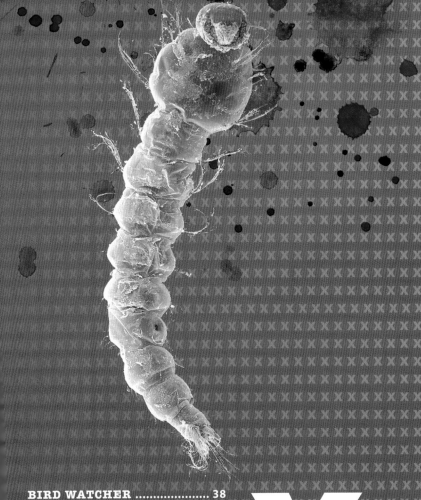

BIRD WATCHER 38

SKEETER SHOOTING 40

KILL THE CARRIER 42

RESOURCES 44

GLOSSARY 46

INDEX 48

Bird-Watcher

Field biologist Sarah Wheeler reveals her secret crush.

SARAH WHEELER has worked as staff research associate at the Center for Vector-borne Diseases at the University of California at Davis.

What does a field biologist do?
WHEELER: We spend a lot of time outdoors. I'm in the field, studying birds. I collect specimens and data that will later be used in the lab.

How do you catch birds?
WHEELER: If we're in a city, we'll set traps. But out in the field, we string these long nets between nine-foot (2.7 m) aluminum poles. They look sort of like volleyball nets. The birds get caught in them. We untangle them and take blood samples. We put bands around their legs so other scientists know they've been tested. Then we let them go.

What do the birds tell you?
WHEELER: When we test their blood, we'll see what birds are carrying West Nile and what their paths of migration are. That can tell us whether the birds got sick somewhere else—or picked up West Nile once they got here.

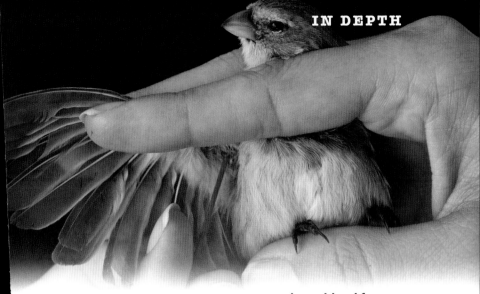

A BIOLOGIST draws blood from a bird to test it for West Nile virus.

Where do you find the birds?
WHEELER: We're looking for places where birds and mosquitoes meet. The first place we went is a lake in California called the Salton Sea. It's a giant polluted lake right in the middle of a desert. It's muggy and buggy and it smells terrible. But I actually have a secret crush on the place.

Why is that?
WHEELER: All these different species meet there—the oddest-looking bugs and birds. Sometimes we catch birds that are weird mixtures. They'll have beaks of one bird and feathers of another. Seeing a bird like that makes my day.

What advice do you have for students who might want to become field biologists?
WHEELER: You have to like being outside. Also, you should get your bachelor's degree in some form of biology. And you can get started right now. Wildlife and conservation groups would love your help.

Skeeter Shooting

Field biologists prowl streets, backyards, and the wild, looking for places where mosquitoes breed. Here is some of the equipment they use.

1 Repellent This is the most important item that mosquito hunters use. They cover themselves—and their clothing—with mosquito repellent to keep the "skeeters" from biting.

2 Loose-fitting, long-sleeved clothing Mosquito hunters wear loose clothing so mosquitoes can't reach their skin through the fabric. Long sleeves and pants keep exposed skin to a minimum.

3 Mosquito traps, dry ice Scientists catch mosquitoes in canvas sacks with screen bottoms and battery-powered fans. The traps are hung overnight next to Styrofoam boxes filled with dry ice. The dry ice changes to carbon dioxide gas, which attracts the

3

KILLERS FOR HIRE

mosquitoes. The fan sucks them into the bags. The bags are gassed to knock out the mosquitoes. Any viruses in their bodies can be studied in the lab.

4 Petri dishes, microscope, glass vials Trapped mosquitoes are emptied onto petri dishes and counted under a microscope. They are sorted by species and placed in vials.

How do governments keep mosquitoes under control?

Many cities, states, and counties have mosquito-control programs. Their purpose is to lower the mosquito population to a safe level and prevent them from out-of-control breeding.

These programs often kill mosquitoes in their young stages—egg, larval, and pupal—before they become biting adults.

Officials keep track of larval and adult mosquito populations. They track the movement of disease-carrying mosquitoes. And they often spray insecticides to kill adult mosquitoes. They might also spray larvicides, chemicals that kill mosquito larvae.

4

Kill the Carrier

These serious diseases are spread by tiny pests.

MALARIA

What is the carrier?

The *Anopheles* mosquito. There are about 400 species of *Anopheles*, but only two dozen of them are carriers of *Plasmodium*, the tiny parasites that cause malaria.

How does it spread?

The mosquito bites a human or another animal that is infected with malaria. The parasites infect the mosquito and mix with its saliva. The mosquito passes the parasites to the next person it bites.

What are the symptoms?

People get fatigue, chills, headaches, and muscle aches. Some have nausea, vomiting, and diarrhea. Malaria can also cause a yellowing of the skin and eyes.

Where can you get it?

Malaria was wiped out in the U.S. in the 1950s. But new cases pop up once in a while. And much of the world is still at risk. In 2018, 93 percent of malaria causes occurred in Africa.

What is the treatment?

There are many medications to treat malaria. If the disease is caught early enough, these drugs can work very well.

Is there a cure?

If you get treatment early, you have a good chance for a full recovery. If you wait too long, this disease can lead to kidney failure, seizures, coma, and death.

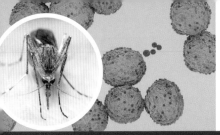
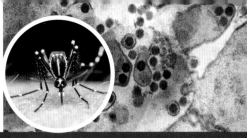

WEST NILE VIRUS	**DENGUE**
Culex mosquitoes are the main vector for West Nile virus, though many other kinds of mosquitoes can carry it as well.	Dengue virus is carried by two species of mosquito: *Aedes aegypti* and *Aedes albopictus*. Just two *Aedes aegypti* mosquitoes can produce as many as 1,600 offspring in a few months.
More than 300 species of birds carry this virus. When mosquitoes feed on infected birds, they pick up the virus. Then they give it to whatever they bite—birds, humans, or other animals.	Mosquitoes get the virus when they drink the blood of an infected human. An infected mosquito can also pass on the virus to its eggs.
About 20 percent of people bitten by an infected mosquito develop West Nile fever. It causes flulike symptoms. Serious complications can include encephalitis, nerve damage, and paralysis.	High fever, headaches, and nosebleeds. Then the patient might begin to bleed internally, which can be fatal.
West Nile is endemic across the U.S. and in much of the rest of the world.	The virus thrives in hot, wet climates where the *Aedes* mosquito populations are high. The disease has exploded in the last 30 years, especially in South America and Southeast Asia.
There is no cure or treatment for West Nile. In mild cases, the symptoms go away in about 10 days. But some people feel sick for weeks.	There is no cure for dengue. Patients who are bleeding internally may need to be given IV fluids or blood transfusions.
Scientists are still trying to perfect a vaccine. But the odds of getting West Nile are very slim. And the chances of dying from it are even slimmer.	The worst symptoms last for about 10 days. A full recovery can take months.

RESOURCES

Here's a selection of books for more information about vector-borne illnesses.

NONFICTION

Abramovitz, Melissa. *West Nile Virus (Diseases and Disorders)*. Farmington Hills, Michigan: Lucent Books, 2013.

DiConsiglio, John. *Blood Suckers! Deadly Mosquito Bites*. New York: Franklin Watts, 2008.

Ford, Jeanne Marie. *Malaria: How a Parasite Changed History (Edge Books: Infected!)*. North Mankato, Minnesota: Raintree, 2019.

Graham, Ian. *Scary Creatures: Scary Microscopic Creatures (Special X-Ray Vision)*. New York: Franklin Watts, 2009.

Markle, Sandra. *Ticks: Dangerous Hitchhikers (Arachnid World)*. Minneapolis, Minnesota: Lerner Publications, 2011.

Simons, Rae. *Bugs Can Make You Sick! (The Kids' Guide to Disease & Wellness)*. Vestal, NY: AlphaHouse, 2009.

Squire, Ann O. *Lyme Disease (A True Book: Health)*. New York: Scholastic, 2016.

Stiefel, Chana. *Animal Zombies!: And Other Bloodsucking Beasts, Creepy Creatures, and Real-Life Monsters*. Washington, D.C.: National Geographic, 2018.

FICTION

Anderson, Laurie Halse. *Fever 1793*. New York: Simon & Schuster, 2002.

Baxter, Roberta. *The Vicious Case of the Viral Vaccine (Galactic Academy of Science)*. Weston, Massachusetts: Tumblehome Learning, 2013.

Giblin, James Cross. *The Boy Who Saved Cleveland*. New York: Henry Holt, 2006.

Haynes, Diane. *Crow Medicine (Jane Ray's Wildlife Rescue Series)*. North Vancouver, British Columbia: Walrus Books, 2006.

Kirchmeier, Kurt. *The Absence of Sparrows*. Boston: Little, Brown, 2019.

London, C. Alexander. *Superspecial: Outbreak (The 39 Clues)*. New York: Scholastic, 2016.

biologist (bye-OL-uh-just) *noun* a scientist who studies living things

carrier (KA-ree-ur) *noun* a human or other animal who carries a contagious disease and can pass it on to others without getting sick

corpses (KORPS-ez) *noun* dead bodies

ecosystem (EE-koh-sis-tum) *noun* a community of animals and plants that depend on one another to maintain a stable environment

encephalitis (en-seh-fah-LYE-tes) *noun* swelling of the brain caused by bacteria or a virus

endemic (en-DEM-ik) *adjective* the term used to describe a disease that will remain permanently in an ecosystem

epidemic (ep-uh-DEM-ik) *noun* a widespread outbreak of disease that affects a large number of people

epidemiologist (ep-uh-dee-mee-AHL-uh-jist) *noun* a scientist who studies epidemics

fatal (FAY-tul) *adjective* causing death

food-borne illness (FOOD-born IL-nuhss) *noun* an illness that occurs from eating food that has been contaminated with parasites such as bacteria or viruses

host (HOHST) *noun* an animal or plant from which a parasite or another organism gets nutrition

infectious disease (in-FEK-shuhss duh-ZEEZ) *noun* an illness that spreads through water, food, air, body fluids, or by carriers

inflammation (in-fluh-MAY-shun) *noun* a condition in which part of the body becomes swollen

insecticides (in-SEK-tuh-sidez) *noun* chemicals used to kill insects

IV (EYE VEE) *adjective* abbreviation for intravenous, which means "entering directly into a vein"

larvae (LAR-vee) *noun* the immature, wingless life-forms that hatch from the eggs of many kinds of insects

migration (mye-GRA-shuhn) *noun* the act of moving from one region or habitat to another, especially according to the seasons

mosquito-borne disease (muh-SKEE-toh-born duh-ZEEZ) *noun* an illness spread by a mosquito

outbreak (OUT-brake) *noun* the sudden spread of disease in a short period of time and in a limited geographic location (like a neighborhood, community, school, or hospital)

paralysis (pur-AL-ih-sis) *noun* the loss of the ability to move (and sometimes to feel) part of the body

parasite (PA-ruh-site) *noun* an organism that lives in or on a host organism and causes harm to the host

perplexed (pur-PLEKSED) *adjective* puzzled or unsure

petri dish (PEE-tree DISH) *noun* a small dish in which microorganisms are grown for research purposes

polio (POH-lee-oh) *noun* an infectious viral disease that harms the central nervous system

pupae (PYOO-pee) *noun* the adolescent life-forms of some kinds of insects; pupae develop from larvae

rabies (RAY-beez) *noun* a contagious and fatal viral disease of some mammals that can be transmitted to humans through saliva

species (SPEE-sheez) *noun* a group of plants, animals, or other life-forms that can mate together to produce offspring

specimen (SPESS-uh-muhn) *noun* a sample

vaccine (vak-SEEN) *noun* an injection of a weakened or killed microorganism given to prevent an infectious disease

vector (VEK-tor) *noun* something that carries a disease from one living thing to another

viral (VYE-ruhl) *adjective* caused by a virus

virus (VYE-ruhss) *noun* a tiny germ that can grow and reproduce only inside the cells of a plant or animal

INDEX

animals, 14, 15, 18, 23, 42, 43.
   See also birds.
Anopheles mosquitoes, 42

birds, 11, 19, 20, 21, 25, 26, 27, 28, 29,
   30, 31, 32, 36, 38–39, 43.
   See also animals.
blood tests, 18, 19, 20, 26, 32, 38, 39, 43
brain scans, 16
Bronx Zoo, 20, 25, 26, 27

carbon dioxide, 23, 40–41
carriers. *See* vectors.
Centers for Disease Control and
   Prevention (CDC), 11, 14–15, 17, 19, 20,
   25, 29, 32
cholera, 15
clothing, 29, 40
Culex mosquitoes, 19, 34, 36, 43

deaths, 15, 20, 21, 25, 26, 27, 28, 29, 42, 43
dengue, 43

Ebola, 15
education, 34, 39
encephalitis, 16, 17–18, 19, 20, 43
epidemics, 14, 15, 17
epidemiologists, 11

field biologists, 38–39, 40–41
flamingos, 20

glass vials, 41
gun violence, 15

H1N1 flu, 15
Hayes, Ned, 11, 12, 17, 20, 26, 31, 32, 34
hosts, 18

infectious diseases, 11, 12, 14
insects, 11, 12

leptospirosis, 15

malaria, 14, 42
measles, 15
medications, 42

microorganisms, 18
microscopes, 18, 41
mosquito-control programs, 41
mosquitoes, 12, 13, 14, 19, 20, 22–23,
   25, 26, 28, 29, 30, 31, 34, 35, 36,
   39, 40–41, 42, 43.
   See also insects; vectors.
mosquito traps, 40–41

New York City, 12, 17, 18–19, 20, 25, 26,
   31–32

outbreaks, 11, 14, 15, 20, 25–26

petri dishes, 41
polio, 14

rabies, 14
recovery, 26, 42, 43
repellents, 29, 40

safety, 29, 34, 41
smallpox, 15
St. Louis virus, 19, 20, 25, 26
survey, 32
symptoms, 19, 28, 32, 42, 43

tools, 40–41
tracking, 14, 41

U.S. Department of Agriculture (USDA), 26

vaccines, 43
vectors, 11, 12, 19, 22–23, 29, 36, 42, 43.
   See also mosquitoes.
viruses, 12, 13, 14, 15, 18–19, 20, 23, 24,
   25, 26, 27, 28–29, 31–32, 34, 36, 38,
   39, 41, 43

West Nile virus, 26, 27, 28–29, 31–32,
   34, 36, 38, 39, 43
Wheeler, Sarah, 38–39